THE TOTALLY AWESOME VAL GUIDE . . .

By Jodie Ann Posserello
as told to
Sue Black

PRICE/STERN/SLOAN
Publishers, Inc., Los Angeles
1982

THANX, I'M SURE

To Lamy, Tanya, Sally & The Girls,
A.P., Warren, John & The Guys,
Bill & Friends of Bload,
J. David & Co., Louise,
and Sensitive Raymond.
And to Moon Unit and P/S/S, fer sure!

Special thanks to Tom Shadyac for permission to use his
"Are You A Valley Girl?" poster material
and to Jenni Kogak, his totally tubular model.

DEDICATION . . . TO MY GANG

A NOTE
TO
READERS

It was like when they asked me to like write this, I thought like Oh, wow, fer sure, someone's really gonna pay ME to tell THEM like how to get it on in the Valley. I'm sure . . . but they did! It blew me away. I got you know, like this super nice check in USA bucks and I was all set to buy like this awesome outfit, a Sergio Valenti, from the Galleria.

Of course, there was the usual hitch . . .
. . . my Mommy Dearest said she'd totally
hemorrhage if I didn't put about 8000% of
it into my "college fund" . . . I am sure!

Well, all this sounds like too easy for
simply writing something, but here I am,
check in hand. Who knows, maybe another
Hemingway . . . Margaux. I'm sure!

Jodie Ann Posserello

CONTENTS

WHERE **VALS** COME FROM

The first thing to understand is that, like, "valley" is a total state of mind. You don't have to live in The Valley to be a Val any more than you have to go to Choate or Vassar to be a Preppie.

It all depends on your basic attitude, y'know? Like, for example, your attitude towards school. Preppies are always trying to get into one. If you're a Val, you're like dying to get out.

Vals come from like all over, you know? Cleveland, Flint, Baltimore, Petaluma. And Texas. Like, the whole state.

CELEBRITY VALS

Even famous people have the attitude sometimes.

For example, RICHARD NIXON was like this total Val, y'know, you could tell. He said, like, "I'm sure" a *lot*. And he did what all Vals dream about doing, which is MOVING TO THE BEACH. Total Val, San Clemente, right near a Howard Johnson's.

DONNY OSMOND, he's got to be one. I mean, anybody who says "Go Hawaiian," I'm sure. Gimme a break. Utah is like in a valley, isn't it?

CAPTAIN JAMES KIRK of "Star Trek." He had the total Val attitude about outer space. I mean, like, he screwed up a few planets. He saved most of them, but he screwed up a few. Which is cool, y'know. Nobody's perfect.

So, like anyplace you have a doughnut shop, or a 31 Flavors, or a semi-decent shopping mall, there are probably a bunch of Vals *right next to you.*

THE MOTHER VALLEY OF ALL VALLEYS

Your basic major valley in California, the San Fernando Valley, is like this totally awesome massive flat place, with all these parts to it.

The Galleria is in Encino, which is this totally *bitchen* part, which has more beauty salons and hair removal places per square mile than like any other place on the planet. The Vals are everywhere, 'cause it's the valley, and like where else would Vals come from?

But, it's a good question: where *do* Vals come from?

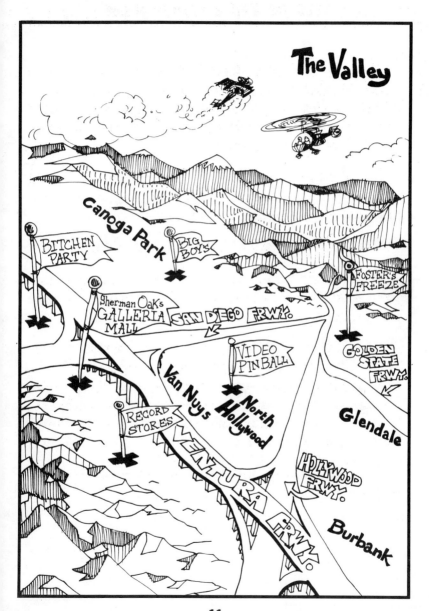

SNUFFING THE MYTHS

Okay, ha-ha, there are these dorky little theories about it, and a book is a good place to like totally get rid of them.

MYTH #1

That somebody like dropped all these weird babies or something, like from helicopters? I'm sure. And like nobody would have noticed?

MYTH #2

That the CIA or someone spiked the food in the places where Val-Parents-of-the-Future used to go on dates. Like maybe Disneyland.

I mean, give me a break, I'm sure, there is like NO WAY.

But in another way, I could like see it, y'know? Because I am not kidding, there are some pretty skanky people running around. YOU NEVER KNOW! That's what Watergate and the Sixties and stuff have taught us.

MYTH #3

That Vals are really these ex-surfers that like crashed into a pier or something, and then migrated inland with their brains scrambled. Well, maybe so. Because inside every Val is like this surfer that's trying to get out.

But anyway, all this stuff is total bull, I'm sure. The Valley was *always* there, the hills were *always* there, and the city was *always* there on the other side. And a Val is a Val. And Vals were always there, too. Except when they were, like, living in New Jersey.

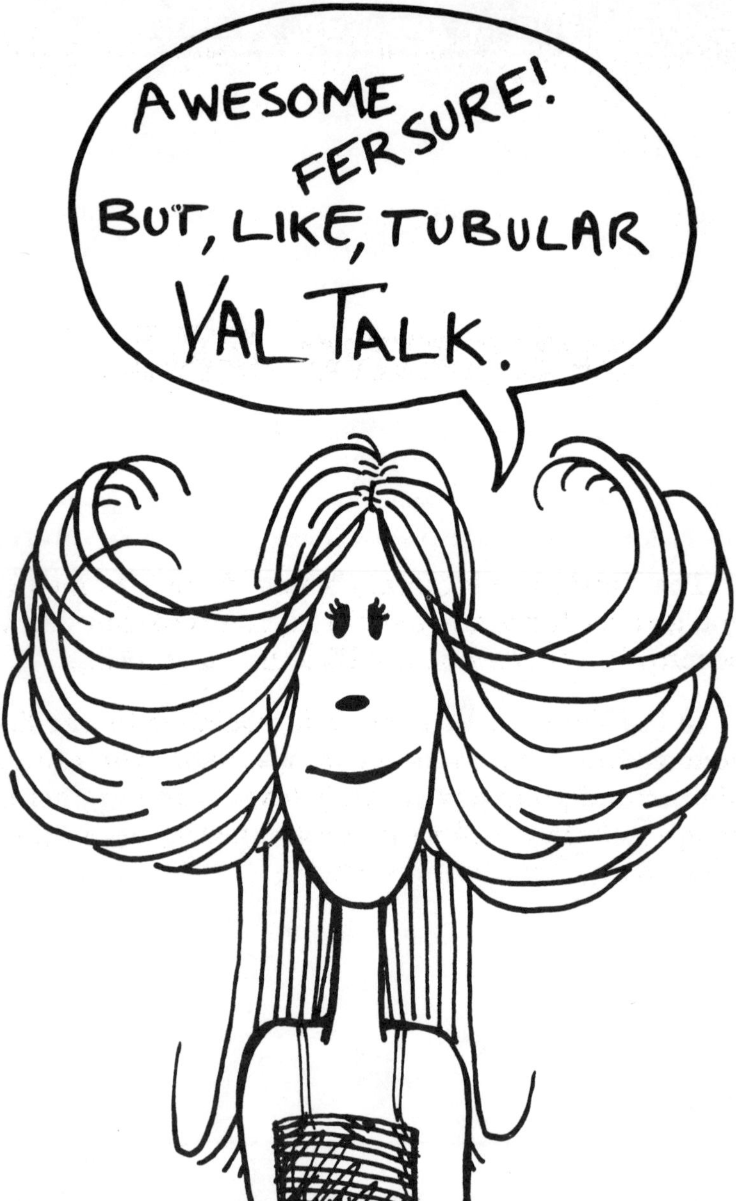
AWESOME FERSURE!
BUT, LIKE, TUBULAR
VAL TALK.

SPEAKING VAL

The Valley is a lot like, y'know, France? I mean, you go over there and everybody has like this weird accent. In the Valley, it's like the same thing.

In the Valley, when you talk, you have to like lie your whole head down on your shoulder and then like extend your jaw *intensely* toward the opposite side, for balance. And be enthusiastic, no matter what. Just, like, *sing* everything.

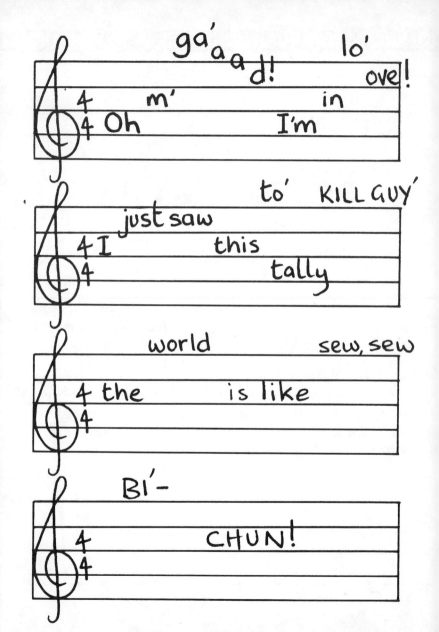

SPEAKING VAL

Val girls talk like they're surprised a lot...and they're always asking questions? The guys hardly talk...they want to act like totally at one with the universe. Or at least the Valley.

That's the big difference between Val Girl Talk and Val Dude Talk. Valley Girls are animated and paint a total scene, using lots of words. Every subject has a connection with their universe.

But the guys! If they can talk at all, and not just snort, they like to use like exclamations or these single words here and there 'cause that's like ultimately cool.

SAMPLE CONVERSATION:

"There was this guy on a motorcycle who freaked out. He didn't wear a helmet and crashed into a Cadillac."

VAL DUDE

Woa! Bummer deal.

VAL GIRL

Ew, gross, I'm sure! Were there like bodies flying all over the place? Oh, that is so grody, I am sure! Like I heard about this guy like cut off his finger, y'know. And he just like started laughing and like threw it away! I'm sure. I'd be like, Oh m'God! Bag that finger! I can't handle this, I'm leaving.

"The driver of the car was all bandaged up, but the guy on the motorcycle just made a dent in the street and walked away."

VAL DUDE

That's kazh.
Gnarly dude.

VAL GIRL

Oh, I am sure. Really? *Really?* Is that the truth? Promise? You lie! He like makes this dent in the street? I'm sure. What was he, like Steel Girder Man or something? You geek, you're lying. O.K., fine, don't tell me. You're just like so totally immature sometimes, you know? I'm sorry, it's like BARF OUT, I hope you're happy you made me like totally sick, I can't even eat this burrito any more. You're totally gross.

YOUR BASIC VAL GLOSSARY

AWESOME -   Unbelievably bitchen beyond description. "Remember the movie 'Alien'? The chestburster?? *Awesome.*"

BABYCAKES -   A male exclamation of pleasure. "I got a tape deck for my pick-up today. Oooh, *babycakes*!!"

BAG IT -   What you do to something (or someone) that's totally gross or offensive. "Look at that bomber zit on your nose! *Bag your face!*"

BARF ME OUT -   See: Gag Me With A Spoon.

BITCHEN -   Probably the best thing you can say about something. Encino is *bitchen* and so are some miniskirts and guys and stuff. *Bitchen* was an awesome word until "awesome" and "tubular" came along. That's evolution, I guess.

BLITZED -   Can you sleep through a rock concert? Do people usually look a little fuzzy? Does your head feel like ginger ale? If so, you know exactly what it means to be *blitzed*!

CARDED - What you get when you try to buy a six-pack and you've got braces and zits.

CRANKING - Something that kicks butt, gets down, goes all out. A good band *cranks* totally.

FER SURE! - The first words a Valley baby learns to speak.

GAG ME WITH A SPOON - See: Barf Me Out.

GRODY - From grotesque. Dirty, messy, disgusting. Like have you ever looked at what's leftover on a plate of enchiladas and refried beans? *Grody* to the max!

I'M SURE - Indicates that you can't believe what you just heard. Vals have an intense feeling for the ironic.

JEL - Someone with a brain made of gelatin. An airhead, but with definite nerd tendencies.

KAZH - Short for "casual," but can also mean "bitchen." Like, "He took me for a ride in this totally bitchen car. It was pretty *kazh*."

KILL -   Somewhere between "bitchen" and "awesome." As in, "I just saw this *kill* movie. Oooh! Had fourteen disasters in it."

LAME -   Dumb, stupid, ridiculous, as in: "I can't see you tonight; I'm waxing my thighs." Pretty *lame*.

LIKE -   The Hamburger Helper of Valley conversation. Goes hand in hand with "Y'know?"

RAG -   What your parents do on you to get you to mow the lawn, clean your room, study, etc. Used most commonly in the form, "My parents won't quit *raggin'* on me." (The appropriate response to this would be "Totally!" or "Fer Sure!")

SCARF/ SCARF OUT -   To stuff your face and like totally consume.

SKANKY -   Weird, sickening, gross. School is a pretty *skanky* place to be.

TOTALLY -
Like "to the max," this means completely, the farthest you can go. For extra emphasis, use both: "God, that outfit is *way totally kill, to the max.*"

TO THE MAX -
What you might as well try to do everything to.

TUBULAR -
Really spectacular. Wonderful and great and awesomely bitchen. There is something slightly cosmic about it, especially to surfers who originated it.

VAL/VALLEY -
Like, a total state of mind, fer sure.

WAY -
A very important word because it exaggerates and emphasizes, which is a key function of any Valley conversation. "That dude is *way* totally bitchen, fer sure. I am not kidding."

HOW TO MOVE
LIKE A **VAL**

In the Valley, nobody moves unless forced to. Like if you're in a record shop and have to get from the cash register all the way back to "W" in the bins, there's no choice—you have to move.

THE BASIC VAL DUDE SLIDE

1. Sit down in a chair and pretend you're in the front seat of a brown metallic Trans-Am.

2. Slide down and lean way back so that the comb in your back pocket is like flat on the seat.

3. Put your foot where a gas pedal would be ... floor it.

THE BASIC SLIDE

**YOU ARE NOW
IN THE CORRECT POSITION
TO BEGIN WALKING!**

WALKING: THE OOZING SLIDE

1. From your Basic Slide position, **MOVE THE CHAIR OUT FROM UNDER YOU.**

2. Plant your feet, tense your arms and begin walking.

3. Keep your legs way in front of your body. Walk like you're balancing a bass guitar on your knees.

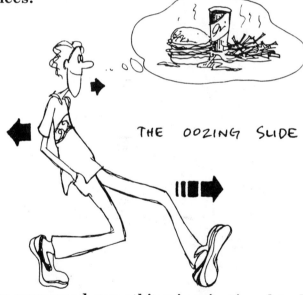

THE OOZING SLIDE

You now need something inspirational to keep you going. Otherwise, you're liable to find a wall to lean against and never move again. Think of a couple of burgers, a large Coke, and fries. Think of heading for them.

HOW TO MOVE LIKE A VAL

The Valley Walk is generally, like, an individualistic experience, but it can be modified for couples.

A Valley girl grabs onto a guy and lets him like drag her around behind him in tiny steps.

VAL DRAG 'N SLIDE

IMPORTANT: A Val girl will gaze up at the guy with total love and adoration, and tilt her head to the side in the basic shoulder-rest position. Not only is this comfortable, but it also allows her to like see around the side of his head to know whether he is looking at like Van Halen records, or mentally tearing the clothes off some other girl.

WHERE VAL POSTURE COMES FROM
• The Telephone Scrunch •

STEP ① DOING THE DISHES

STEP ② SAYING HI

~ MOM & DAD ~

HOMELIFE

VALLEY PARENTS

Val parents are like regular Vals that got old and forgot how to drive fast.

WHERE VAL PARENTS CAME FROM

Val kids have always been there, but Val parents came from like Cleveland or Scranton or Tulsa. And they're wandering around the Valley mumbling, "Who am I," "Where am I," "Where am I going," and "Where can I get a good Maine lobster?"

There are three major ways in which Val parents calm down. If you learn them, you can get your parents to stop bashing you around for smashing the car up again.

Most Val parents will respond to:

1. Going to K-Mart and buying three dozen tube socks on sale.

2. Going to marriage encounter weekends.

3. "Joining In."*

*Joining In is like attending PTA meetings or church socials or neighborhood anti-bussing rallies. These are places where they make new friends. When they get enough of them, they have a barbecue.

Valley parents can do disturbing things like building $25,000 swimming pools in the backyard, then just wading around in the shallow end holding a cocktail. Or they'll tell you your bikini is too small, then go "JOINING IN" at a nudist bridge club or something. Bizarre? Totally.

WATER SPORTS
WITH MOM

ROLE MODELS

Val parents are always trying to be, like, role models, but unless you want to grow up to be a professional barbecuer you'll need outside help. Here's a list of outside role models. Even if they don't live in The Valley, they probably have a valley state of mind.

DUDES

Bo & Luke Duke

Leif Garrett

Doug Henning

Matt Dillon

Shaun Cassidy

GIRLS

Brooke Shields

Jamie Lee Curtis

Cindy Garvey

Everybody in the Miss America Pageant

Shaun Cassidy

FAMILY ROLE MODELS

Eight Is Enough

The Brady Bunch

The Big Valley

General Hospital

VALLEY HEROES

Charles Bronson

Clint Eastwood

Steve Garvey

Ted Nugent

The Thing

A GUIDE FOR THE PERFECT VAL PARENT

My mother is always saying to me, like, "What do you *want* from me??" in this, like, soprano voice. So I made up this list of the bitchenest things and gave it to her, to sort of like guide her:

THE PERFECT VAL PARENT...

. . . lets you borrow the credit cards, but doesn't ask for the receipts.

. . . issues a separate allowance for albums.

. . . won't lock up the liquor cabinet at your parties.

. . . hires a maid for the really grody housework.

. . . covers for you when school calls about your 182 absences from class.

. . . won't get upset about totally trivial matters such as grades, curfew, or your boyfriend's motorcycle.

So I gave this list to my mother and she like shoved me into a closet. So like it doesn't always work.

Keys to Mom's Mercedes
*"Such a bitchen car,
y'know."*

Dad's Credit Cards
*"Like I never leave
home without them."*

Manicured Nails
*"My maid, you know,
does the dishes."*

A VAL'S ROOM

The most important place in the whole house is your room. It's like a sanctuary from the world and even other Vals. It must have:

1. **A PHONE**
   (Even in a sanctuary you shouldn't lose contact.)

2. **STEREO PLUS HEADPHONES**
   (A necessity, especially if your parents are into like Elvis; Crosby, Stills & Nash; or the first Rolling Stones albums.)

3. **POSTERS EVERYWHERE**
   (Blank walls are like so gross. For dudes, Ted Nugent, AC/DC, and Blue Oyster Cult. For girls, Scott Baio and Rick Springfield. Everyone can have a Jim Morrison poster.)

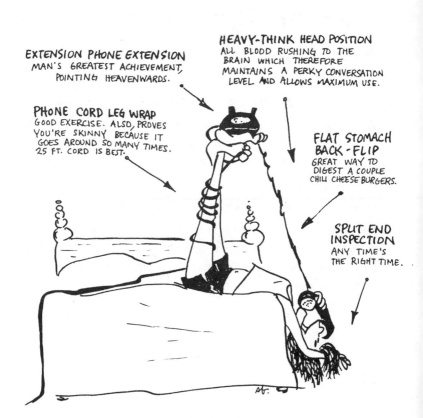

HEAVY-THINK HEAD POSITION
ALL BLOOD RUSHING TO THE
BRAIN WHICH THEREFORE
MAINTAINS A PERKY CONVERSATION
LEVEL AND ALLOWS MAXIMUM USE.

EXTENSION PHONE EXTENSION
MAN'S GREATEST ACHIEVEMENT,
POINTING HEAVENWARDS.

PHONE CORD LEG WRAP
GOOD EXERCISE. ALSO, PROVES
YOU'RE SKINNY BECAUSE IT
GOES AROUND SO MANY TIMES.
25 FT. CORD IS BEST.

**FLAT STOMACH
BACK-FLIP**
GREAT WAY TO
DIGEST A COUPLE
CHILI CHEESE BURGERS.

**SPLIT END
INSPECTION**
ANY TIME'S
THE RIGHT TIME.

How TO TALK ON THE PHONE

WHAT TO DO IF YOUR PARENTS LEAVE TOWN

(This is like potentially the best thing that could ever happen to you.)

Before...

1. Make sure they leave you a bunch of money. Tell them, like, "What if something happens? What if the house blows up?" Your mother will freak out, and probably throw in a couple of credit cards, too.

2. Get them to put your kid sister in a hotel.

During...

1. As soon as they leave, get the car keys from where they hid them and go cruise.

2. Get the dirty books from where they hid them and read them with your friends.

3. PARTY.

After...

If you have any money left over, use it to like leave town. When your parents get a look at what you've done to the house, your life isn't worth a pair of tube socks.

Wavy, Long Hair (Optional) •
"But like totally shorter on top."

Heavy Makeup •
"To like hide the zits, gag me!"

Betty Boop Smirk •
"Like I'm so-o-o cute."

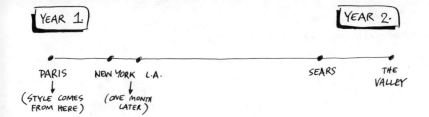

YEAR 1.

YEAR 2.

PARIS
(STYLE COMES FROM HERE)

NEW YORK L.A.
(ONE MONTH LATER)

SEARS

THE VALLEY

VALLEY STYLE

If you're a Val and you're not into cute styles, then you're probably, like, dead.

HOW TO GET STYLE

THE two most popular ways to get style:

1. Master Charge
2. Visa

Once your pocket is stuffed with credit cards, head for the Galleria. After that, simply buy all the matching outfits you see in the window.

THE ADVANTAGE OF VALLEY STYLE

Valley girls like to dress "in the now." Of course, "now" in the Valley is like "then" everywhere else. Which is great, because it means that you can go anywhere in the world and not have them think you're some kooky trend-setter or something.

Thin Head Band
"Like I own 15 of these, you know."

Complete Accessories
*"My jewelry is like worth,
I dunno, so-o-o much money."*

**Flowered, Polka Dot, or
Ruffled Blouse**
*"It like makes me look
so-o-o-o chesty."*

Stylish Belt
"It looks totally gnarly."

**Pac-Man Underwear
(Optional)**
"I'm like into clean stuff."

Fashionable Miniskirt
*"You know, like it still
hides the grody baby fat."*

Ankle Socks
"I dunno, they're like in."

BEAUTY AND GROOMING
THE MORNING ROUTINE

You get up in the morning, you look in the mirror, you freak out...those are the first steps in your morning routine.

Then you must give yourself plenty of time to fix all the damage your body was doing to your face all night long. Get it down to a science:

1. WASHING YOUR FACE (SPECIAL ANTI-ZIT SOAP)

This has, like, little rocks in it that help you wake up through the total pain method.

2. PUTTING ON YOUR MAKEUP

Use lots and lots since your mother will make you wash half of it off anyway.

EYESHADOW: sparkly purple

ROUGE: sparkly peach

LIPGLOSS: totally

Don't rub anything in. Let the colors really show. Your face should like stand on its own two feet.

3. BLOW DRYING YOUR HAIR

This is the most important function of the day. One wrong blow and you walk around looking like a total geek.

the BLOW-DRY MELTDOWN

4. GETTING DRESSED

    Wear your frilly blouse and your prairie skirt with the ruffles, or your new capri pants. Always think Val.

5. PHONING A FEW FRIENDS

    Ask each one if they think you're fat. They'll say no. Have a couple of brownies and you're ready to face the day.

BEACH STYLE: GOING FOR IT

God. Surfer Girls, y'know?? They all have this like mile-long straight blonde hair, and these total tans.

In the Valley, girls try to grow their hair long, but the smog like chokes the follicles or something, and your hair freaks out and you get all these split ends and stuff. So-o-o grody!

BEAUTY TIP

What you do in this case, is you like curl the ends in this sausage shape around your head. Like, in the morning, with your curling wand. So like even though you've got these fully grody split ends, they get hidden.

BEAUTY HAZARD

Okay, you always wanted to go mega-blonde, so you gotta use this bleachy-type stuff on your hair. But be careful. One important phone call, you forget it's on your head, and you end up looking like a DANGER sign on the highway.

the HOLLYWOOD BLEACH-OUT

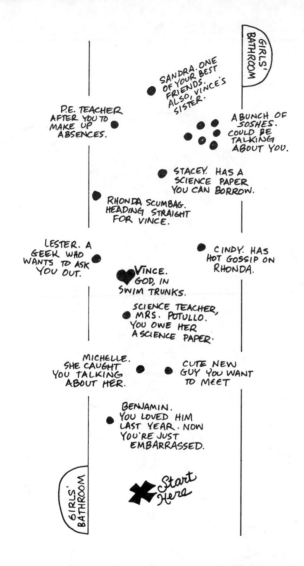

SAMPLE HALLWAY COURSE

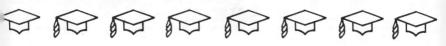

SCHOOL

Except for the part where you have to go to class, school can be like almost bearable.

WHAT YOUR PARENTS WANT

Parents want you to go to school so someone else can nag you for a while and put you through the kind of dumb routines that are supposed to prepare you for life and make you as miserable as they are.

SCHOOL

THE SCHOOL ROUTINE

1. Get up super-early.
2. Go there.
3. Sit in grody classrooms and do all this garbage.
4. Go home.
5. Do more garbage.
6. Go to sleep.

So that's like so-o-o unhealthy, I'm sure! School life is like this totally gross existence. Like if it were Star Trek or something, you'd be one of the planets that Kirk had to save, I'm sure, except he'd probably have to like blow up your parents and most of the teachers and stuff, to put them out of their misery.

But there is another side...

WHAT YOU WANT

You want to take advantage of the bitchen things school has to offer: hallways, new guys, and information on who did what with whom. You want school to realize its full fun potential. Start by creating a new routine:

THE REVISED SCHOOL ROUTINE

1. Get up eventually.

2. Go there.

3. See people.

4. Ditch class.

You can't do it that way everyday because they'll call out the Feds or something, but at least it's an option. Vals try to make the best of every situation.

THE MAIN FUNCTION OF SCHOOL

The main function of school is to provide you with a hallway for, like, social discourse. The hall is where you get all the really important information. Walking down the hallway is exactly like cruising the boulevard, except that running into people won't raise your insurance rates.

HOW TO DO THE HALL

The trick is to like talk to as many people as possible before running into someone you hate. It is an extremely intense social situation.

A good trip down the hallway can take anywhere from like five minutes to half an hour. If you're a pro, you can spend the whole day there.

For best results, the hall should be like packed to the max with bodies. Preferably those of guys on, like, the swim team.

1. Standing at one end, spot somebody you know way down at the other end. Wave like you're flagging down a rescue boat in the Pacific. (SEE FIRST HALLWAY POSITION)

— FIRST HALLWAY POSITION —

2. Approach your friend and stand there (SECOND HALLWAY POSITION).

   Use one of the following conversation starters:

   - "You got that mini? I was going to get that mini, and you got that mini."

   - "I am in total love. Something happened. I have to talk to you like right away!"

   - "You should hear what Babette said about you and Todd. It's like the biggest cut."

   - "Mr. Rosenquarts goes out with boys."

   Any one of these is sure to like spark her interest and get your conversation going full blast.

-SECOND HALLWAY POSITION-

3. **Now Look Around.**

   You'll see Babette, Todd, the guy you're in love with or Mr. Rosenquarts like standing right there . . . you didn't notice them. Go into THIRD HALLWAY POSITION and say, "OH MY GOD!! I can't beLIEVE it, iamsucha GEEK, why didn't you TELL me!" Then say your friend's name a lot, as if you were dying of malaria: "Oh, Debbiedebbiedebbiedebbie!"

– THIRD HALLWAY POSITION –

4. **Primp your hair and head for the bathroom (FOURTH HALLWAY POSITION)**

   Combing your hair is the best way out of any embarrassing situation.

—FOURTH HALLWAY POSITION—

SCHOOL

THE CAFETERIA

The only other decent place at school is the cafeteria. While the hall serves as an information exchange, the cafeteria is the place for reflection, evaluation and like meaningful discussion.

Start by getting a good place near the door and discuss each person who walks by:

● "He's got tall hair. He must have had, like, a head operation under his hair."

● "Oh m'God! Here comes Carla Lipscome. She's the one I lost my Todd to. Don't look at her, you'll turn to scum!"

● "Look at him...look at the way he's looking at me. ...he wants me."

● "He is such a geek. I mean we're talking nerd, mas grande."

● "She says she has a problem with baby fat. It's more like elephant fat! How gross."

● "There goes Cindy's boyfriend. I could have him anytime, but I don't, like, steal guys. We went out a few times, but that's different."

You can feel like totally at home in the cafeteria. You can do practically anything you want there. Just don't eat the food.

SCHOOL

SPORTS

School sports are supposed to be like this big bitchen deal, but in the Valley getting up in the morning is about as physical as anyone really wants to get.

Some Vals are into like beach sports. Like for guys there's Beating Up Surfers (and Running Away when things get hairy), and for girls there's Tanning and Bikini Waxes (bag that body hair).

Other typical Valley sports are like:

Bowling	Limited movement, air conditioning and a snack bar; it's pretty tubular.
Video Games	You can score like a million points and spend the whole day without moving an inch.
Track & Field	Take your pick-up and like leap over the train tracks and into a field before the train gets there. Way bummer if you miscalculate.
Chug-A-Lugging	How much beer can you drink without stopping? This is like the total Val Olympic Event.
Cheerleading	Little minis and spirit dots. Rah-rah, I'm sure. Gag me with a spoon!

SCHOLASTIC GOALS

Popularity is like the one goal that most Vals strive for. So, you like want to get yourself on the yearbook staff. Then, you can put pictures of yourself all over the place, and in the index after your name will be about 72 page numbers. This makes it look like you were this totally bitchen person, doing all these pep-rally type things, when most of the time you were really just blitzed out of your mind, listening to your radio in the bathroom. Image and achieving popularity are what school is all about.

HOW TO SIT THROUGH CLASS

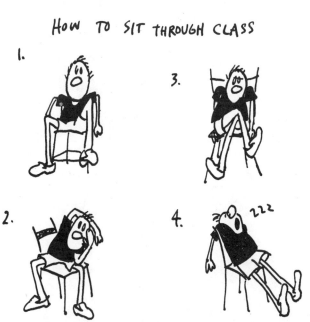

Cauliphone Ear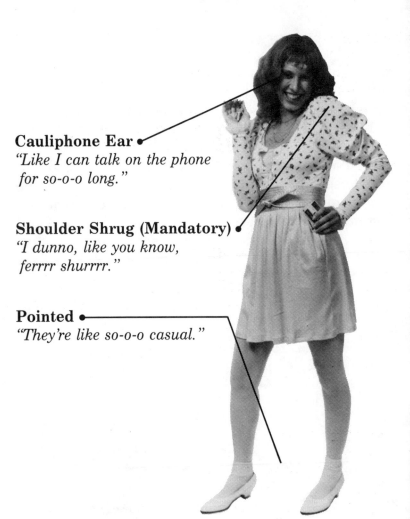
*"Like I can talk on the phone
for so-o-o long."*

Shoulder Shrug (Mandatory)
*"I dunno, like you know,
ferrrr shurrrr."*

Pointed
"They're like so-o-o casual."

HANGING OUT

To be a Val is to be, like, *restless* with *cravings*. You have to like get moving, but only long enough to go someplace where you can like *stop*. A true Val never wants to move for too long.

GREAT PLACES TO HANG OUT AND NOT MOVE

1. **The Beach ...**
    where you like lie down.
2. **The Movies ...**
    where you can sit down in the dark and let the actors do all the moving.
3. **The Car ...**
    where you just relax and let it move you.

SURF HUNGER

If you're a Val, you like wake up every morning of the summer and go, "Oh m'God, it's like 118 degrees outside and I am like, y'know, dying!"

There is not Breeze One coming through the window, and if you're watching like Family Feud or something? You're like sweating and everything, and like sticking to the couch? I'm sure, barf OUT. You're like, "Gag me, THERE MUST BE MORE TO LIFE THAN THIS." So your brain starts like pondering SURF.

Vals have this deal where they like *love and crave* the surf, y'know? And the total Val heartbreak is that that's where they want to come from. Like, the beach. But they can't, cause they're Vals, and it's like the worst thing that ever happened to them. They're like *emotionally distraught,* y'know, because they need the beach, and they're always trying to surf, but they have to like drive so far to get there.

There is one bad thing about the beach, though. The locals.

LOCALISM

Okay, it's like: You know how Russia hates America? Well, it's the same thing. I mean, the locals like have this thing in their head like, *"My beach, my wave."* Well, I am so sure! And, they like paint on all these garbage cans in Santa Monica: VALS GO HOME. And then they expect the Vals to like throw their empties and stuff in them y'know? I am sure! I wouldn't support any garbage can that like *insults* me, no way.

BUMMER.

HANGING OUT AT THE GALLERIA

For the most awesome place to hang out, of course, you head for the Galleria. The Galleria has mass quantities of *everything*: little places to eat, movies, bitchen clothes stores and shoe stores, plus video games, and like even escalators that do the moving for you.

You could like go to the Galleria, live your life and die right there, and it would be like, O.K., fine!

One of the most awesome responsibilities of a Valley Girl is learning how to shop the Galleria. The day you buy your first mini is like your coming of age, so it's important to know what you're doing.

WHEN IN DOUBT... SHOP

HOW TO GET A MINI AT THE GALLERIA

First, get two of your friends to go along because you, like, need their opinion.

Then:

1. TRY ON EVERY SINGLE THING IN THE STORE. . .because what if you didn't and you missed something?*

THE ADVANTAGE OF SHOPPING WITH FRIENDS....

*Your friends will yell at you to hurry up. Just yell back: "Come on, I'm sure, I always wait for You-ou!"

2. Get everyone's opinion. Then no matter what anyone says, BUY THE OUTFIT DISPLAYED IN THE WINDOW. After all, who knows more about style than the people who decorate windows?

This means you get:

The top	The mini
The little socks	The little slippers
The earrings	The bracelets
The blusher	The shadow

and probably some really cute underwear and a couple of albums to go with it all.

Your mom will totally understand because she, like, taught you to shop this way.

After about a zillion hours of shopping, you and your friends will be pretty tired. That's when it's time to find a bathroom and brush your hair (which you've been doing all over the store, anyway.)

THE BATHROOM HANG OUT PROCEDURE

(This method works at theaters and concerts, too. Anywhere they have a bathroom.)

1. Go in and immediately like glue yourself to the mirror.

2. Take out your brush, your comb, your little makeup case, and your radio. Put all of these on the counter. Turn on the radio.

3. Discuss everybody's hairdo and give thorough explanations about split ends and roots. Take time to laugh about the beasty hairdo on the saleswoman in the dress shop.

4. Absolutely *die* because the saleswoman walks in.

O.K., now the best part:

5. Talk guys, and like how far everybody *goes*.

6. Lie.

After the bathroom, you can go back outside and like hang over the railing and look at the geeks on the lower levels. Talk about them.

OH M'GOD!

... SACRIFICING COMFORT FOR STYLE.

OTHER HANG OUTS

MOVIES

Go to a movie that you've seen a few times so you can start up a conversation and keep it going all through the film and not miss anything. Talk to the actors on the screen, and tell them when they're about to blow it. Scream and laugh and throw popcorn when they do.

ROLLER SKATING RINKS. . .

Never go to a rink if you want to truly roller skate. Everybody is showing off and you can't, like, get around. Like every 15 minutes they have a snowball dance, and you take your life in your hands. Just walk around in groups, feather your hair, and discuss guys.

FAST FOOD PLACES

Great hang outs if you have a car. Double chili-cheeseburgers are certain death fer sure, but with an afterlife.

DOUBLE
CHILI
CHEESE

AMUSEMENT PARKS

Not bad if you stay off the rides. You can always pick-up on a cute ticket taker.

ROCK CONCERTS

These include everything that's great about the other hang outs, but with live music! Plus, for a couple of days afterward you can relive the entire experience in your ears. It *is* cool. The gift that, like, keeps on giving.

T.V. AT HOME

Glue yourself to the couch and become at one with Star Trek.

EASY-ACCESS PHONE IN BENEVOLENT AUTHORITY POSITION.

LOWER JAW EXTENSION ALLOWS FOR MINIMUM MOVEMENT.

KNEE-CHIP HUG WITHIN REACH OF EITHER HAND.

TOE EXTENSION VOLUME CONTROL DEMANDS EXCELLENT TOE MUSCLE TONE, OR SET MAY BE TURNED OFF. THEN WHAT?!

CAT REST FOR OVER-EXTENDED TOES.

How To WATCH T.V.

WHEELS

Cars are like the total
essence of Valley life.
Even if you have nowhere
to go, you can't get there
without a car.

WHEELS

Your driver's license is your like passport to coolness. Without it you are a mere chuckhole in the highway of life. Consider your existence without a license:

PARENTS:

You are like totally subject to their weirdness. Like, if you want to go cruising, they take you to Marineland and put you on a boat ride.

FRIENDS:

You are forced to get in with an older crowd. You live life in the fast lane, but with a retainer in your mouth. Totally embarrassing.

PUBLIC TRANSPORTATION:

You wait about a million years just to cram yourself into a metal box with about a zillion strangers. And for this you pay money.

UNCONTROLLED MODES:

Such as skateboards, roller skates, and bikes. (Although it *is* intense to bomb down the street on a chopped skateboard with sheepskin lining.)

HOW CARS ADD TO YOUR LIFE

Cars can like give a whole new meaning to an otherwise dull existence.

EMOTIONALLY:

Driving around at 80 m.p.h. in a totally hot metallic brown Firebird with a bitchen stereo blasting, nobody will guess what a truly boring person you are.

CREATIVELY:

From working on cars, you know how to turn a Cadillac Coupe de Ville into a pick-up truck, or a city garbage truck into a home for four.

POLITICALLY:

You can express your opinions on current events with bumper stickers. And you can like hang out the window and scream at buildings, pedestrians, and other drivers.

ROMANTICALLY:

Guys — even if a girl doesn't like fall in love with you, there's a chance she'll like fall in love with your car. Girls — even if a guy doesn't like fall in love with you, you can always get him to like fix your carburetor.

HOW CARS CAN DETRACT FROM YOUR LIFE

There's a bad side to even the best things. A car can cause problems. Like, the financial considerations can have a heavy impact on your life:

1 dented fender (minor) = 3½ - 4 miniskirts.

1 cracked windshield = 2 season's worth of shoes.

1 imploded bumper and grill = outfits for 3 bar mitzvahs.

1 new paint job = 1 year's supply of albums.

1 engine overhaul = 3-year's playing time at a video arcade.

1 totaled car = your entire social life, forget it.

One wrong move in a car can make you useless to the planet and to yourself.

THE VALLEY DRIVING TECHNIQUE

Valley girls cruise for like short distances, like from store to store. They're pretty good at parking and stuff, but murder on the open road.

Drive the same way you talk: Involve lots of people but don't pay a whole lot of attention.

1. Ignition: Slant your head towards your right shoulder and like concentrate.

2. Release the brake: Open your mouth and look up at the sky.

3. Gas it: Go real fast, screaming and laughing.

4. Slam on the brakes after you go through a red light.

5. Stall: Roll your eyes far in your head so that your friends can't see them anymore, and sigh heavily. Say, "I can't believe I just did that! I swear to God I did not see that light! I swear to God I did not see that light! That light was not there the last time I went down this street. I am like freaking out, totally."

6. Resume: Your friends will make you feel better telling you they just saw God, and he was driving a Trans Am. Everybody screams, and you follow him for about half an hour, using steps 1 to 5.

GUYS WITH CARS

A Valley Dude invests his life in his car. He'll hop it up, chop it, ride it high, put massive wheels on it, equip it with an intense stereo system, paint it metallic, give it a vinyl roof and hope to, like, even drive it down the street some day.

WHO'S WHAT - A GUIDE TO CRUISING

If you're cruising down the boulevard, that is, if you found one the cops didn't block off, you gotta know *who* you're gonna find in *what* type of car. Otherwise, you could end up following a total nerd for hours.

HOW TO RIDE IN A CAR
WITH YOUR BOYFRIEND

FIREBIRD/MUSTANG/CAMARO Either cheerleaders or the fast crowd. There are three or four of them, and at least one isn't wearing any underwear. Tube tops and jeans. Roach clip hanging from the rear view mirror. Great tans. Looking for guys.

MAZDA Girls named Vicki or Janine, who just got their eyebrows re-shaped. They have a little diamond set into the nailpolish on their index finger, and they are on their way to brunch.

DATSUN Mr. Slick wearing a leather jacket from Casa de Suede. Going into his father's real estate business. Scheduled to report in to about fifteen friends tonight.

WHEELS

MACH 1 The god who won "best body," and his girlfriend, who is scummy, which is the only reason he's with her and not me.

TOYOTA CELICA FASTBACK A girl named Donna who is on her way back to Beverly Hills to register for silver at Bullocks. She is not engaged, but why wait? She has her father's company gas card.

CORVETTE A surfer who took like the wrong turnoff, and totally regrets it.

VAN At least two guys. They have surf hunger. Gauze curtains on the windows, sunset painted on the outside. Plush carpeting. A sexmobile. May hook up with the girls in the Firebird.

EL CAMINO or DODGE PICK-UP Three guys with long hair and a couple of moustaches between them. They're drinking beer out of a plastic Pepsi bottle or something. Smoky atmosphere.

BMW ("Beemer") A guy in a Fila jogging suit, going to a hot tub party at his shrink's house in Malibu. Beachboys blasting on the Blaupunkt.

SCIROCCO A totally bitchen car, because it is driven by me, Jodie Ann Posserello. I'm like only 15½, but my dad got it for me to practice on. He's sitting next to me, having about 40 heart attacks.

PORSCHE Stolen. From a Preppie.

CHECKPOINTS FOR CRUISING

You are probably listening to the right cruising music if . . .

. . . the car like jumps around because your feet are tapping a beat on the accelerator.

. . . your d.j. gives regular surf reports, even though you live in Oklahoma.

. . . the music sticks around after you turn the radio off.

CULTURE TIP

Don't listen to punk. Punks are like grody to the max. They have the worst taste! Like, why have a mohawk when you can feather your hair?

ON THE LOOKOUT FOR GOD

VALS IN LOVE

Vals fall in love all the time, just like anybody else, all over the place, and every chance they get. I am not kidding, one good cruise down a fully-packed hallway and you could like fall in love for life.

There are like differing philosophies on the subject, y'know? Like, Valley girls always want to fall in love. They're falling in love about once every twenty minutes. On the other hand, valley guys are totally kazh about everything. I asked this one dude to like describe the perfect girlfriend? And he goes, "Sure. None." And I'm, like, O.K. fine! God, I was so offended.

VAL DATING

The Valley is like intensely romantic. Neon lights from the all-night taco stands filter through the smog and you get, like, this bitchen glow!

Most Val dating falls into one of two categories:

1. You go to like Magic Mountain and go on all the hairy rides, or you go see a movie, which if he picks it, will probably be just like totally violent and gross; or you go to some great hang-out where all your friends are, and let them see you with God, walking around with your hands in each others' back pockets.

OR

2. You just shine all that and go park somewhere. That's the way a date can like start out kazh and end up kill. Totally. Fer sure.

FALLING IN LOVE TIP

Okay, this is like really important. This is what you should like carve into your memory for life:

DO NOT EAT BEFORE YOU MEET
OR TALK TO ANY GUY

Like, once I was at the beach, and I was fixing all the strings on my bikini, which takes about five minutes. It's a bitchen bikini, but I have to say it does give you this really stupid-looking tan.

Anyhow, my best friend Debbie had these herb bars. And I was on a diet and like starving to death, so I figured, well, health food, y'know? So I ate about ten of them.

And then who comes along but God himself, this Babe-Totale. And he says "Ooh, Beh-beh! What's happnin?" And like what's "happnin" is that I've got all this herb breath and about forty tan lines from strings, and I'm like this giant Triscuit on the beach.

And so God starts talking to Debbie, and they go off to the pier to get chiliburgers. My friend Debbie, the health addict. I am sure.

So take it from me. Don't eat before you talk to guys. And like stay away from health food while you're at it.

ON TRUE LOVE

Valley girls get together for slumber parties and stuff, and dream of the day when they'll meet God. Like once, I had this dream about a guy named Kelley. I loved Kelley. He totally knew I loved him. I loved him last year, and we had Kelley Day. We had everything green, because he's, like, Irish? We had green streamers, green cake, green everything. it was like very, very strange. And everybody went to the bathroom green the next day, because we used so much green dye. I was like, "Oh. I am so *sure*."

But now, this year, I know the truth. And the truth is that the only sexy guy in my school is on page 72 of the yearbook. He's God. I've looked at his face so many times it makes me ill.

Like, that's how life is when you're a Val.

BEING **VAL**

You can walk, talk and look like a Val, but unless you can like think on your feet and duck embarrassing questions or situations, you'll never make it.

The object here is to like confuse the person who's ragging on you long enough so you can, like, take off. Or at least get him to say, "Will You disappear!"

PARENTS

You and your friends ate all the food for my barbecue! There's nothing left! What do you have to say for yourself?

You told me to clean the refrigerator. You're never satisfied.

You crashed the car? You crashed the car? How could you crash the car?

I couldn't help it. Like I think it was fate.

What's the idea of coming home at 2:30 in the morning?

I figured if I stayed out later, you'd get upset.

Why can't you ever lift a finger to help around here?

I totally hurt my finger doing homework.

What's wrong with you? Why do you act this way?

It's my skin problem. It takes up a lot of my time.

SCHOOL

Why were you absent from school yesterday?

I forgot. I thought it was Saturday.

Why were you late to class today?

I thought today was Sunday. But then I remembered.

Your paper on recombinant DNA is late.

I've been in France.

It says here you have to go to the orthodontist every day this week. That brings your total P.E. absences to 83. Isn't that a little strange?

No, Ma'am. It's pretty normal for me.

FRIENDS

Where's the ten bucks you owe me?

Ow! God, I got beer in my cut! Ooh, Beh-beh! I'm blacking out.

Where did you get all those zits?

They aren't zits. I inherited like a disease or something.

Why did you see "Endless Love" 14 times?

(Sorry. No excuse)

STRANGERS

You've caused quite a bit of damage here to my car. I hope you have insurance.

Oh, absolutely. But it's like French insurance so like I dunno . . .

So you're a Val, huh?

Response #1: No way!

Response #2: I don't *live* there. My parents do. I live with my parents.

OR

Response #3: Totally. I was born there. At the age of birth.

Why do you live in the valley?

I live in the valley because it *is* cool.

What's so cool about it?

Me.

EPILOGUE

Okay, so like now you've finished the book. It was so-o-o awesome getting it all together, but now for the important stuff — like tell your friends to buy this book. There's a bitchen sale on at the Galleria and I'm running low on bucks.

This book is published by

PRICE/STERN/SLOAN
Publishers, Inc., Los Angeles

whose other splendid titles include such literary classics as:

**MOON ZAPPA'S OFFICIAL VALLEY GIRL
COLORING BOOK**

**MURPHY'S LAW (AND OTHER REASONS
WHY THINGS GO ƆNOᴚW!)**

MURPHY'S LAW/BOOK TWO and BOOK THREE

HOW TO BE A JEWISH MOTHER

HOW TO BE AN ITALIAN

and many, many more

They are available at $2.95 each wherever books are sold,
or may be ordered directly from the publisher by sending a
check or money order for the total amount plus $1.00
for handling and mailing. For a complete list of titles
send a *stamped, self-addressed envelope* to:

PRICE/STERN/SLOAN   *Publishers, Inc.*
410 North La Cienega Boulevard, Los Angeles, California 90048